COUNT ON ME
Sports

Powerful Stories of
PERSEVERANCE
in sports

BRAD HERZOG

"As shown by the wonderful stories in Count on Me: Sports, athletics can not only reveal character, but also inspire it."
—**Shannon Miller,** two-time Olympic gold medalist in gymnastics

"The true tales in Brad Herzog's books show how the games we play can teach seriously important life lessons."
—**Jake Delhomme,** former Super Bowl quarterback for the Carolina Panthers

free spirit
PUBLISHING®

Library of Congress Cataloging-in-Publication Data
Herzog, Brad.
  Powerful stories of perseverance in sports / Brad Herzog.
     pages cm — (Count on me: sports)
     ISBN 978-1-57542-456-9 (paperback) — ISBN 1-57542-456-8 1. Athletes—Conduct of life—Juvenile literature. 2. Athletes—Biography—Juvenile literature. 3. Sportsmanship—Juvenile literature. 4. Character—Juvenile literature. I. Title.
  GV697.A1H3966 2014
  796.092'2—dc23

                                                                                          2013049152

ISBN: 978-1-57542-456-9

Reading Level Grade 5; Interest Level Ages 8–13;
Fountas & Pinnell Guided Reading Level V

Edited by Alison Behnke
Cover and interior design by Michelle Lee Lagerroos

Cover photo credits: background © Bruxov | Dreamstime.com;
clockwise from top left: AP Photo/Scott A. Miller; Cal Sports Media via AP Images; AP Photo/Kevin Larkin; AP Photo/Damen Jackson via Triple Play New Media; Press Association via AP Images; AP Photo/Greg Wahl-Stephens. For interior photo credits, see page 102.

10 9 8 7 6 5 4 3 2
Printed in the United States of America
S18861116

Free Spirit Publishing Inc.
6325 Sandburg Road, Suite 100
Minneapolis, MN 55427-3674
(612) 338-2068
help4kids@freespirit.com
www.freespirit.com

DEDICATION

For Judy Mozersky, who continues to persevere and inspire.

ACKNOWLEDGMENTS

Thank you to Judy Galbraith, Margie Lisovskis, and the rest of the crew at Free Spirit Publishing for having the courage to pursue a series of books celebrating stories of character in sports. I found Alison Behnke to be both insightful and inclusive as an editor, an author's dream combination, and Michelle Lee Lagerroos put in overtime making sure the designs were just right. Finally, I am grateful to Aimee Jackson for bringing me to Free Spirit in the first place and for her unwavering support and friendship.

CONTENTS

INTRODUCTION 1

UNHITTABLE 5
BASEBALL • NEW YORK, NEW YORK, UNITED STATES • 1993
When life throws a pitcher a curveball, he tosses a no-hitter.

BEAUTY IN MOTION 9
TRACK AND FIELD • ROME, ITALY • 1960
A young woman overcomes a tough start to become
a track superstar.

HEART OF A WINNER 15
GOLF • LEÓN, MEXICO • 2011
Two organ transplants don't stop a golfer from
achieving his dreams.

DECIDING TO SOAR 19
FENCING • WEST PEABODY, MASSACHUSETTS, UNITED STATES • 1976
With the help of self-belief and a sword, a girl
discovers her potential.

THE FIGHT OF HIS LIFE 23
BOXING • LOS ANGELES, CALIFORNIA, UNITED STATES • 2011
A boxer's biggest bout is the fight for his reputation.

RELENTLESS RACER...27
HANDCYCLING • LONDON, ENGLAND • 2012

One man could have let a horrific accident end his racing
career. Instead, he simply changed his course.

CHANNELING STRENGTH..31
SWIMMING • ENGLISH CHANNEL • 1926

A long-distance swimmer who refuses to quit
becomes "Queen of the Waves."

MOVING FORWARD..37
BASKETBALL • BRISTOL, CONNECTICUT, UNITED STATES • 2011

A top basketball player takes on her most
challenging opponent.

EYES ON THE PRIZE...40
DISTANCE RUNNING • SYDNEY, AUSTRALIA • 2000

Being legally blind won't keep this runner from competing.

C IS FOR COMEBACK...46
BASKETBALL • GETTYSBURG, PENNSYLVANIA, UNITED STATES • 2012

A college basketball player returns to make a very big point.

"JUST SKATE"...51
SPEED SKATING • LILLEHAMMER, NORWAY • 1994

A speed skater has one last chance to turn heartbreak
into heroics.

ON TARGET 55
ARCHERY • MASSA-CARRARA, ITALY • 2005
An unexpected new challenge doesn't stop a world-class archer from aiming to be the best.

CONQUERING A CONTINENT 59
CROSS-COUNTRY SKIING • ANTARCTICA • 2012
One woman challenges herself in the most unforgiving place on Earth.

THE MATCH THAT WOULDN'T END 63
TENNIS • WIMBLEDON, ENGLAND • 2010
Two men compete like champions in the longest match in pro tennis history.

FINISHING TOUCH 69
TRACK AND FIELD • BARCELONA, SPAIN • 1992
Sometimes finishing a race last is the most impressive feat of all.

HARD TO TAKE DOWN 73
WRESTLING • PHILADELPHIA, PENNSYLVANIA, UNITED STATES • 2011
Perfection is within reach for a wrestler born with one leg.

FACE TIME 77
WHEELCHAIR BASKETBALL •
NEW BRIGHTON, MINNESOTA, UNITED STATES • 2010
An athlete in a wheelchair rolls into the pages of *Sports Illustrated*.

LITTLE GIANT 83
FIGURE SKATING • SARAJEVO, YUGOSLAVIA • 1984
Illnesses keep threatening to bring down a figure skater,
but he always rises up again.

TECH TRIUMPH 87
BASKETBALL • WINSTED, CONNECTICUT, UNITED STATES • 2008
After 265 straight losses, a girls' basketball team
maintains a winning attitude.

HIS NAME IS PRIDE 91
BASEBALL • MONTREAL, CANADA • 1993
A baseball player who was born hearing impaired
works his way to the major leagues.

SELECTED BIBLIOGRAPHY 95

INDEX 97

ABOUT THE AUTHOR 103

INTRODUCTION

In 2005, when motocross racer Ricky James was 16 years old, he crashed during a race. James was thrown headfirst from his Yamaha YZ80. He crushed his spine, broke his wrist and a couple of ribs, and had a collapsed lung. He spent seven hours in surgery. Afterward, doctors told him that he would never walk again. He would be paraplegic—paralyzed from the waist down.

Not walking wasn't what worried James the most. "I didn't think about never walking again," he said. "The only thing that mattered to me was that I couldn't race anymore." It turns out he was wrong. Within a year, James had adapted a hand-cranked bicycle to racing.

But James's world had changed forever. He adapted to life in a wheelchair. That meant figuring out new ways to do what were once simple tasks—showering, getting dressed, tying his shoes. At the same time, he set some very big goals. Within three years of his accident, he began competing in triathlons. These three-part races include swimming, biking, and running. First, James had to learn how to swim. "I wanted to pick up a new challenge," he said. "I wanted to prove that I was an athlete."

Only a few months later, James traveled to Hawaii for the Ironman World Championship. He used his new swimming skills to cover 2.4 miles in the ocean. He rolled along for 112 miles in his hand-cranked cycle. Finally, in an adapted race chair, he completed a 26.2-mile marathon. Twelve hours and 44 minutes after he started, he crossed the finish line.

It would be an impressive feat for anyone. For a young man who had fought for his life only a few years earlier, it was inspiring. Of course, Ricky was just staying true to the word tattooed on his right leg. It read: PERSEVERANCE.

The stories in this book celebrate that word in all its forms. Perseverance is defined best by the people who display it. It can mean courage and strength, as shown by the wrestler who became a champion—even though he only had one leg. Or perseverance can mean toughness, as in the story of the golfer who had his heart replaced twice but never lost his spirit. It can translate into grit and determination, displayed by the boxer who was wrongly imprisoned but never gave up the fight for his freedom. Or it can mean the bravery and the resolve of the woman who swam across the English Channel. Perseverance can appear in the form of endurance, like the tennis players who didn't back down, even when their match took three days. Sometimes it means strength of mind, as shown by the fencer with dyslexia who turned newfound self-esteem into gold medals.

All of these stories share two important things. They all feature obstacles that seemed to stand in the way of reaching a dream. And they all feature amazing athletes who show us that it is possible to overcome nearly any challenge. Whether it's on the speed skating track, the pitcher's mound, or the frozen lands of Antarctica, these tales of perseverance are about people and possibilities.

UNHITTABLE

SEPTEMBER 4, 1993 • NEW YORK, NEW YORK, UNITED STATES

It was a Saturday afternoon in Yankee Stadium. New York Yankees pitcher Jim Abbott stood on the mound and stared at his catcher. In the stands, the fans cheered themselves hoarse. The Yankees were in the midst of a pennant race, but that's not what had the crowd in a frenzy. So far, not a single batter for the Cleveland Indians had managed to get a hit. At age 25, Abbott was on the verge of making history.

Then again, he already had.

"I believe you can do anything you want if you put your mind to it," Abbott likes to say. Growing up in Flint, Michigan, he had set his sights on making it to the major leagues. He wanted to be called a big leaguer. Instead, he was called cruel names. Some kids nick-named him "crab" because he was born without a right hand. But Abbott figured he would just have to become a one-handed baseball star. "A few people told me that I wouldn't go far in sports," he said. "I didn't listen."

In high school, Abbott became the starting quarterback and punter on his school's football team. He was even better in baseball. Playing first base, shortstop, and left field, he batted .427 as a senior. In 1985, he was selected by the Toronto Blue Jays in the amateur draft. But instead of joining the minor leagues, he decided to go to college. At the University of Michigan, Abbott became a national sensation—as a pitcher.

To pitch and also field from the mound, Abbot had to make a tricky series of moves. With a left-handed baseball glove where his right hand would be, he pitched with his left hand. After he threw the ball, he switched the glove onto his pitching hand. To make a fielding play, he cradled the ball and glove in the crook of his right arm. Then he grabbed the ball and threw it with his left hand. Some opponents tried to take advantage of Abbott's system. In one high school game, a team bunted eight times in a row. But Abbott became a very good fielder. He threw out seven of those eight bunters!

In three seasons pitching for Michigan, Abbott had a 26–8 record. In 1987 he received the James E. Sullivan Memorial Award as the nation's top amateur athlete. He then earned a spot on the U.S. Olympic team. At the 1988 Summer Olympics, he pitched the team to a gold medal.

Abbott's success didn't stop there. Next, the California Angels (now the Los Angeles Angels)

SWITCH HIT

Growing up, Shay Oberg watched Jim Abbott pitch in the big leagues. Despite having been born without a left hand, Oberg herself was a star Little Leaguer. She went on to be a high school star, too. As a senior in Billings, Montana, she earned all-state honors. At the plate, Oberg batted from a left-handed position. She used her right arm to slap at the ball with a backhand stroke. She hit well, but she couldn't generate much power. So she worked harder. She also tried new things. In college, where she played for Montana State University Billings, she decided to experiment as a switch-hitter. That meant she batted left-handed against right-handed pitchers and right-handed against left-handed pitchers. In 2008, as a junior, she hit three home runs—all of them right-handed. As an opposing coach said, Oberg showed that "anybody can do anything if they want to work hard enough."

drafted him in the first round. He was finally a big leaguer, just like he'd dreamed. As a major league rookie, he won 12 games. The best of his 10 big league seasons was 1991. That year, he won 18 games for the Angels. But the Yankees-Indians game, two years later, was his most memorable.

With the crowd cheering him on, Abbott hurled the ball toward the plate. The batter slapped a ground ball to the shortstop, who scooped it up and threw it to the first baseman. "He did it! He did it! No-hitter for Jim Abbott!" shouted the announcer. Abbott's teammates crowded around him in joyful celebration. By then, he was no longer viewed as a great one-handed pitcher. He was just a great pitcher. Period.

BEAUTY IN MOTION

SEPTEMBER 8, 1960 • ROME, ITALY

The odds were stacked against Wilma Rudolph from the beginning. She was born into poverty in rural Tennessee, along with 21 brothers and sisters. She had several serious diseases as a child, including scarlet fever and polio. Her battle with polio left her nearly unable to use her left leg for several years. When she grew up in the 1940s, African Americans were often treated like second-class citizens. Black women struggled to find opportunities and acceptance in sports.

With these challenges in her path, what were the chances that Rudolph would become an Olympic hero? How likely was it that buildings, schools, and highways would be named after her? Would anyone

DREAM RUN

Billy Mills grew up poor, living on the Pine Ridge Indian Reservation in South Dakota. Mills was a member of the Oglala Lakota tribe. He became an orphan at age 12. Before Mills's father died, he gave his son some advice. He said, "You have to look deeper, way below the anger, the hurt, the hate, the jealousy, the self-pity, way down deeper where the dreams lie. Find your dream. It's the pursuit of the dream that heals you." Mills took these words to heart. He went to college and became an All-American distance runner. Then he earned a trip to the 1964 Summer Olympics in Tokyo, Japan. There, to the crowd's amazement, he came from far behind to win the 10,000-meter gold medal. In that race, Mills also set an Olympic record and ran 50 seconds faster than he had ever run before.

have predicted that bronze statues and postage stamps would bear her image?

"Beauty in motion" is how her former track coach described her. But as a child, Rudolph didn't *feel* very beautiful. She wore a leg brace and a special shoe to help her walk. "I remember the kids always saying, 'I don't want to play with her. We don't want her on our team.' I never forgot all those years," she said, "when I was a little girl and not able to be involved."

However, there never seemed to be a hurdle that this future sprinter couldn't overcome. Baseball pioneer Jackie Robinson himself once gave her some advice. He said, "Don't let anything, or anybody, keep you from running."

Rudolph's weak left leg made running seem like a distant goal. So for several years, she tried to strengthen her leg. She did physical therapy. First, she did this once a week at a distant hospital. Then she learned to do it at home. Finally, by the age of 12, she could walk without leg braces or crutches. She kept working hard to get even stronger. In high school, Rudolph was a four-time all-state basketball player. She also became a track star. She won state titles at three distances—50, 75, and 100 yards. And at 16 years old, she made the U.S. Olympic team. She earned a bronze medal in the 4 x 100-meter relay.

Still, there were more hurdles. Rudolph had hamstring injuries in 1958 and again in 1959. These injuries caused her to miss most of the track season at Tennessee State University. Even 1960 started poorly: Rudolph had to have her tonsils removed.

But 1960 also happened to be the first year the Olympic Games were televised throughout much of the world. And that meant that it was the year Wilma Rudolph emerged as an international superstar. In the 220-meter run during the Olympic trials, Rudolph set a world record. She arrived in Rome, Italy, for the Summer Games with high hopes. When she got there, she found more hurdles in her path. A sprained ankle the day before her first race? No problem. Rudolph won the 100-meter dash by nearly 3 meters. Rain during the 200-meter finals? Ho-hum. She won again. Finally, on September 8, she was anchoring the last leg of the 4 x 100-meter relay. She was far behind. So she kicked into high gear and chased down her competitors. Rudolph became the first American woman to win three track and field gold medals.

Unfortunately, there was one thing that could stop Rudolph. At the age of 54, she died of brain cancer. Not long after her death, the Women's Sports Foundation created a special award. It would be presented annually to a female athlete. Each winner would have overcome hard times, worked hard for success, and served as an inspiration and role model. Could they have named it after anyone else? It's the Wilma Rudolph Courage Award.

HEART OF A WINNER

JUNE 26, 2011 • LEÓN, MEXICO

Golf is a sport of mental energy. It takes focus, confidence, and often a bit of courage. You could say it requires heart—or, in the case of Erik Compton, three hearts.

Growing up in Florida, Compton was good at baseball and football. But at age nine, he was diagnosed with a disease that limited his heart's ability to pump blood. He was put on a transplant waiting list for a new, healthy heart. In February 1992, doctors replaced the 12-year-old's diseased heart. Compton's new heart came from a 15-year-old donor named Jannine. She had been killed by a drunk driver.

Compton still wanted to be an athlete. But he was too weak now for contact sports like football. So he turned to golf. As he put it, this sport allowed him to

"go out and not think about the issues I have." And Compton was great at golf. He became a college star at the University of Georgia, a member of the U.S. amateur Walker Cup team, and a two-time winner on the Canadian Tour.

The average life span of a donor heart is about 10 years. Jannine's heart lasted 16 years. But in 2007, Compton suffered a heart attack. He was 27 years old. He managed to drive himself to the emergency room, where he collapsed. Eight months later, he underwent a second heart transplant. It was a 12-hour procedure. This time the donor heart was from a former college volleyball player named Isaac. He had died in a motorcycle accident. "I still think of them as part of me," said Compton of Jannine and Isaac. Compton is also on a mission to encourage people to be organ donors.

For a while after the second transplant, Compton figured his golfing days were over. He didn't think his body could handle the sport's activity. But he missed the sport. Soon he started watching golf on TV. He imagined playing again. He pictured himself in the place of the winner. As he got comfortable with a mental return to the game, he started to think his body could take the challenge, too.

Six months later, Compton decided it was time to try playing in a pro tournament again. But he was still too weak to walk far. So he used a golf cart. The tournament was called the Children's Miracle Network Classic. For someone who had been through as much as Compton had, the name was appropriate. "It really is a miracle what I've been able to achieve," Compton admitted. His surgeon, Dr. Si Pham, agreed. Dr. Pham said it was "unheard of for a patient to be playing sports on a national level like this."

In fact, Compton started playing better than ever. In 2010, he got to compete in his first major championship—the U.S. Open in Pebble Beach, California. A year later, on June 26, 2011, he won the Mexico Open. That victory meant he would achieve a lifelong dream. He qualified to compete in 2012 as a full-fledged member of the PGA Tour. In 2013, he even finished fourth in a PGA tournament called the Honda Classic.

Four-time major championship winner Phil Mickelson, for one, is in awe of his fellow golfer. "It's not what you accomplish in life, it's what you over-come," he said. "Erik's accomplishments are incred-ible, given what he's overcome." Compton knows that he might need another new heart in the future. And each time he has surgery, the risks are greater. But he says, "I would never really change my life because I've experienced so much. I've been able to drive through things. I just keep plugging away."

After all, he insists, the length of a life isn't what really matters. It's the quality.

DECIDING TO SOAR

1976 • WEST PEABODY, MASSACHUSETTS, UNITED STATES

When Molly Sullivan Sliney was in fourth grade, she made a bad decision.

Sliney had a learning disability called dyslexia. That meant she had a hard time reading and spelling. When it came time for a spelling test in front of her class, she thought she was ready. After all, she'd spent the whole week studying. But when the teacher gave her the easiest word on the list, she got it wrong. As she sadly walked back to her desk, she heard her classmates laughing. One of them whispered that she was "too dumb to be in this class."

Looking back on the moment, Sliney saw that she had two options. She could ignore what people said about her. Or she could agree with it. "I made the wrong choice," Sliney often says, as she speaks to students all around her native Massachusetts. "I started to believe what they said." She began to lose her self-esteem.

Sliney's father decided to do something to lift his daughter's spirits. He had noticed how she enjoyed holding a foil—a sword used in the sport of fencing. Sliney loved to pose with a foil as if she were one of the Three Musketeers leaping into battle. So her father signed her up for fencing lessons. Sliney's teacher was a fencing coach and retired firefighter named Joe Pechinsky. In the kitchen of West Peabody's fire station, Pechinsky wrote Sliney's name on a blackboard. She had lost so much confidence that she could barely look him in the eye. But then, chalk in hand, he turned the letters of her name into a piece of art. He drew a proud and beautiful peacock. Pechinsky looked at her and said, "If you believe in yourself, this is what you can become. Be anything. Do anything. Go anywhere you want."

Sliney thought hard about Pechinsky's words. She'd already believed negative things about herself. This time, she decided to believe something positive.

With Pechinsky as her coach, Sliney worked hard. She got better and better at fencing. Within a few years, she made her first national fencing team. A few years after that, she earned a full fencing scholarship to the University of Notre Dame.

With Notre Dame's team, Sliney won 160 of 174 bouts and earned two national foil fencing titles. She was also named the university's Female Athlete of the Decade for the 1980s. Then, after graduating with a degree in marketing, she did go places. As a member of the U.S. Olympic fencing team, she traveled to Seoul, South Korea, in 1988, and Barcelona, Spain, in 1992. In Seoul, Sliney cried as she watched the Olympic flame being lit. "It hit me then about the road I had taken to get to the Olympics. For the first time, I realized how far I had come," she said. She also competed in the Pan-American Games, winning two team gold medals.

Years later, Sliney came full circle. Once again, she stood in front of a group of students in a classroom.

Everyone's eyes were on her. Only this time, Sliney was sharing her story.

When Sliney talks to kids, she tells them how her accomplishments were possible. She says that the secret to her success was her self-belief and her decision to set goals and work toward them, one step at a time. "When someone says something positive about you, you have two choices. One choice is to believe them. The other choice is to ignore them," she tells the students. "That day in the fire station, I made the right choice."

THE FIGHT OF HIS LIFE

OCTOBER 15, 2011 • LOS ANGELES, CALIFORNIA, UNITED STATES

In 1983, at age 24, Dewey Bozella was convicted of a crime. He was found guilty of breaking into the home of a 92-year-old woman and killing her. The judge sentenced Bozella to 20 years to life in New York's Sing Sing Correctional Facility. But Bozella hadn't committed the crime. He was innocent.

23

Bozella had already had a very tough life. He grew up in Brooklyn, New York. At the age of nine, he watched as his father beat his pregnant mother. She died from her injuries. A few years later, Bozella's older brother died after being stabbed in a fight. As a teenager, Bozella moved to the quieter town of Poughkeepsie, New York. There he developed as a talented amateur boxer. But a few months later, he was arrested for murder. The only evidence against him came from local criminals who claimed he did it.

During his first few years in prison, Bozella was bitter. "Every second, every day, every year, every decade, there's no hope," he said. Then he discovered the prison's boxing program. "Boxing's my savior," he explained. "It helped me find the freedom I needed." Eventually, Bozella became Sing Sing's light heavyweight champion.

In 1990, Bozella got a retrial. The other side's lawyer offered him a deal. If Bozella admitted that he was guilty, he could walk out of the courtroom a free man. Bozella had already been in jail for seven years. He desperately wanted out. But he refused. He said, "You're not going to make me say something I didn't do." Somehow, despite no physical evidence against him, he was found guilty again. Bozella went back to prison.

Bozella was knocked down, but he kept fighting. During the day, he trained as a boxer. At night, he focused on getting an education. He earned a college bachelor's degree. Then he earned a master's degree. He also wrote weekly letters to the Innocence Project. This organization works to free people who have been wrongly convicted. After five years, the Innocence Project finally took Bozella's case, only to discover that police had destroyed any evidence. But a couple of hard-working lawyers heard about the case and took it on. Eventually, they determined that the original witnesses had been lying. Bozella had been framed.

In October 2009, Bozella stood in the same courtroom where he had been convicted twice. He had spent more than a quarter-century behind bars. In this room, Bozella was finally freed. "A man's reputation is everything if he's fighting for something that's a worthy cause," he said. "My worthy cause was my freedom."

Bozella used his freedom to work with teenagers. He taught them about the benefits of boxing and the dangers of gang life. He had another dream, too. He had always hoped to fight in one professional boxing match. After hearing his remarkable story, boxing promoters made it happen. They set up a bout on October 15, 2011. Bozella faced a pro named Larry Hopkins. Bozella, who was by then 52, had a famous fan in his corner—President Barack Obama. The president had called to wish him luck.

Hopkins was 22 years younger than Bozella. But the older boxer was better. After the four-round fight, Bozella was the winner. "A dream come true," he called it. Then again, he had already won his biggest battle.

RELENTLESS RACER

SEPTEMBER 5, 2012 • LONDON, ENGLAND

Alex Zanardi was back in a familiar place. It was a road-racing course known as Brands Hatch in London, England. Zanardi had first competed there 21 years earlier. Back then, he was a young man driving one of the world's fastest machines. Now, more than two decades later, the experience was very different. This time, he had no race car. And he had no legs.

Once, Zanardi had been one of the world's best drivers of open-wheel cars. These cars are built specifically for racing. They are very lightweight and usually have only one seat. The wheels are located outside the main body of the car. And these cars go *very* fast—sometimes more than 200 miles per hour.

In 1997 and 1998, Zanardi was the points champion in the Championship Auto Racing Teams (CART) series. He also raced in dozens of Formula One events with some of the world's speediest vehicles. But in 2001, it all came to a crashing halt. During a race in Germany, Zanardi was in a terrible accident. His car spun into a competitor's path. The other car sliced right through Zanardi's vehicle at a terrifying speed. Zanardi lost both of his legs and nearly died.

So what does a racer do when his legs are amputated? He finds other ways to race.

Zanardi managed to race again by using hand-operated controls to drive his car. Within two years, he was back on the track where he'd crashed. He completed the final 13 laps that he had missed because of his accident. His average speed? More than 190 miles per hour. Soon, Zanardi started competing in the World Touring Car Championship. His special race car allowed him to drive using his artificial legs and feet. He won four races that way!

Zanardi eventually retired from auto racing. He soon found another way to compete. He discovered something known as a handcycle. It's a three-wheeled, hand-powered, fast-moving vehicle. Zanardi began racing in the handcycling division of marathons.

Once again, Zanardi was a world-class competitor. In Italy, he won the handcycling versions of the Venice Marathon and the Rome Marathon. In 2011, he was the winning handcyclist in the New York City Marathon. The following year, he earned a spot on the Italian team that would compete in the 2012 Summer Paralympics. That's how Zanardi found himself back at the Brands Hatch course in London. And that's how he won three medals. He earned two golds in individual races and silver in a team relay. "It shows that I am a complete cyclist," Zanardi said, "even if I have no legs."

Zanardi doesn't really like the word *disability*. He prefers to call it *diverse ability*. In fact, his own diverse ability is what makes him most proud. At that 2012 Paralympics, his teammates chose him to carry Italy's flag during the closing ceremony. Later Zanardi described his experience at the Paralympic Games. He said, "I found happiness the very first day of training. It would have been worth doing even if I had won nothing here."

CHANNELING STRENGTH

AUGUST 6, 1926 • ENGLISH CHANNEL

Gertrude Ederle set off on a long swim toward England one morning in 1926. The eyes of the world were upon her. That very morning, a London newspaper declared on its front page that women were athletically inferior to men. The article argued that promoting female competitive sports was a waste of time. So Ederle swam off to set the record straight.

She had been a swimming star since her childhood in New York. At age 12 (when she was known as Trudy), she showed she could go fast. She broke the women's world record in the 800-yard freestyle. At age 14, she showed she could go far, winning a three-and-a-half-mile race. By the time she was 17, she had collected more world records than birthdays. The next

year, she won a gold medal and two bronze medals at the 1924 Summer Olympics.

In 1925, when Ederle was 19 years old, she made an announcement. She said she wanted to swim across the English Channel—something no woman had ever done. The channel is a 21-mile-wide body of chilly water between France and England. It has been called "the Mount Everest of swimming."

On her first try, Ederle was more than two-thirds of the way across when she stopped to spit out salt-water and float for a while. Her trainer was on a support boat next to her. When he saw her stop, he thought she was in trouble. He pulled her from the water, which meant she was disqualified. Ederle was bitterly disappointed.

So she tried again, one year later. On August 6, 1926, Ederle jumped into the channel in France.

Covered in lard for warmth, she started swimming. It was a rainy, blustery day. The weather caused currents so strong that many steamship crossings were canceled. Ederle had hours and hours of swimming ahead of her. But after only about seven minutes, she was hit by a very strong wave. She almost quit. "But I thought I had to make a showing," she said later. "So I just kept on and on and on."

CROIZON'S CROSSING

The English Channel has continued to be a challenge for swimmers. In 2010, it was the site of another first. Forty-two-year-old Frenchman Philippe Croizon became the first limbless person to swim the channel. Croizon lost a large portion of all four limbs after an electrical accident in 1994. "Two solutions were offered to me: to die or decide to live. I chose to rebuild myself," he explained. While in the hospital, he watched a TV documentary about crossing the channel. He thought: "Why not me?" Sixteen years later, he did it. He used artificial legs and flippers to propel himself. And he completed the feat in almost the same amount of time as Gertrude Ederle had 84 years earlier.

The water was so choppy that Ederle couldn't swim in a straight line. Her wobbly path turned a 21-mile crossing into a nearly 35-mile challenge. It was so dangerous that at one point her trainer called for her to come out of the water. Ederle's reply, which newspapers worldwide soon printed, was, "What for?"

Until Ederle's swim, only five people—all men—had ever succeeded in swimming across the channel. The fastest of these swimmers made the crossing in 16 hours and 33 minutes. When Ederle finally came ashore on the English coast that evening, her time was a little more than 14 hours and 30 minutes. She was exhausted but thrilled. "I *knew* I could do it," she told reporters. "I *knew* I would, and I *did*."

When Ederle got home, New York City honored its "Queen of the Waves" with a ticker-tape parade. About 2 million spectators cheered for the swimmer. But for Ederle, those cheers were muffled. She'd had poor hearing ever since having measles as a child. Possibly as a result of the channel swim, her hearing grew progressively worse. By the 1940s, she was completely deaf. This, too, was just a challenge to overcome. Ederle, who lived to be 98, spent much of her life teaching swimming to hearing impaired children.

MOVING FORWARD

APRIL 11, 2011 • BRISTOL, CONNECTICUT, UNITED STATES

In April 2011, University of North Carolina senior forward Jessica Breland went to ESPN's studios in Bristol, Connecticut. She was there to take part in the WNBA draft. One by one, players' names were called. Maya Moore. Amber Harris. Danielle Robinson. Twelve picks came and went. The first round was over. And Breland was still waiting.

Two years earlier, a pro career seemed to be the next step for the 6-foot-3 star. She had just finished her junior season. She had topped the team with 14 points, 8.5 rebounds, and 3.1 blocked shots per game. Her highlights included a 31-point outburst against Oklahoma and a 23-rebound performance against Duke. Playing in the WNBA seemed like a sure thing.

But all that changed one day in May 2009. After having chest pains and breathing problems, Breland went to the doctor. She had an exhausting series of

37

tests. And she got shocking news. Breland had Hodgkin's lymphoma, a form of cancer. Within a few days, she was getting chemotherapy. She endured these treatments every two weeks for the next six months. Side effects included aches, chills, fatigue, nausea, and a constant metallic taste in her mouth. She lost 25 pounds. Her hair thinned, and her skin began to turn a sort of purplish color. "I went from being a basketball player to a person with cancer," she said. But she had one goal: *I'm going to beat this*.

When she finished the treatments, she got some *good* news. Her doctors said that her body was cancer-free. The disease might come back someday, but for now, she was healthy. "I can't wait to get back on the court," she said at the time. "I'm feeling pretty good, really good." Sitting on the bench next to the coaches during the 2009–2010 season, she had learned a lot. But her toughest challenge was getting back into physical shape. "My mind was moving faster than my body," she said. She also had scar tissue on her lungs. So she had to go in and out of games at first until her lungs could get used to the pace. Still, she kept working her way back. That season, Breland averaged 12.4 points and 7.1 rebounds for North Carolina.

Through it all, the WNBA was in her sights. "I just want to be able to go from growing up and watching it," she said, "to being able to play in it." So Breland waited that day in April 2011, hoping to hear her name called during the pro draft. That would mean that her dream of becoming a professional basketball player might come true.

Then, with the first pick in the second round, the Minnesota Lynx selected . . . Jessica Breland. She was in the pros!

Breland was the 13th overall selection in the draft. In this case, 13 certainly wasn't a lucky number. But that's only because it wasn't luck that got Breland to the WNBA. It was grit.

Before the 2011 season began, the Minnesota Lynx traded her to the New York Liberty. Later, she would play for the Connecticut Sun. Whatever the team, Breland played with guts and determination.

In addition to achieving her WNBA dreams, Breland has also helped others. She works with an organization supporting cancer research and treatment for young cancer patients. Her goal is to give these kids the chance to pursue *their* dreams. Naturally, she calls it the Jessica Breland Comeback Kids Fund.

EYES ON THE PRIZE

SEPTEMBER 30, 2000 • SYDNEY, AUSTRALIA

Marla Runyan cannot see the tape at the finish line. But she knows how to get there.

Runyan is legally blind. As a distance runner, she can vaguely make out the track beneath her feet. Her competitors are blurs of color, but she can often tell them apart by their running style. And she still has vision from the corners of her eyes. So when she sees a cluster of officials at the side of the track, she knows she has reached the end of a race. Often, she's the first one there.

Runyan's accomplishments would be impressive for any track and field athlete. For someone who can no longer see the large "E" on the eye exam chart, they are even more remarkable. In 1992, she earned four gold medals at the Paralympic Games, for athletes with a range of disabilities. Runyan won her Paralympic golds in events from the 100-meter dash to the long jump. In 1999, she won the 1,500-meter gold medal at the general Pan-American Games. In 2003, she won her third straight outdoor 5,000-meter national title. Three years later, she won the Twin Cities Marathon. Plus, in the midst of all those feats, Runyan competed in the Sydney Summer Olympics. She was the first legally blind American athlete to take part in an Olympic Games.

In 1978, when Runyan was nine years old, she was diagnosed with Stargardt disease. This eye condition grew progressively worse. It basically left her with a blank spot in her central vision. Contact lenses helped, but her eyesight was still very poor. And it was getting worse.

As her vision faded, Runyan had trouble in school at first. But with the help of visual-aid tools and

audiobooks, she went on to do very well. "My mother once told me, 'Marla, there is nothing you can't do, but everything is going to take you twice as long,'" she explained. "Time was the limiting factor for me. I wasn't dumb—I was just slow."

But Runyan soon became known for her speed. When it came to sports, Runyan's first love was soccer. However, as her vision worsened, it was too hard for her to see the ball. She didn't give up sports. She just tried new ones. In high school, she set a school record in the high jump. She used reflective tape to help her find the bar. In college, she competed in the seven-event heptathlon. The heptathlon's parts are the 800-meter run, javelin throw, long jump, 200-meter run, shot put, high jump, and 100-meter hurdles. Runyan couldn't see the hurdles, so she carefully counted her steps between leaps.

At the 1996 Olympic trials, Runyan finished 10th in the heptathlon. In the process, she set a national record in the 800-meter run. So she decided to focus only on the running events. Four years later, in Sydney, Australia, Runyan was a member of the U.S. Olympic team in the 1,500 meters. She made it to the finals

ATTEMPTING THE UNCOMFORTABLE

Like Marla Runyan, Aaron Scheidies was born with Stargardt disease. He slowly lost his eyesight. "I don't even remember what full vision looks like because it was so long ago," said Scheidies, who turned 32 in 2014. "I just see moving blobs." Yet Scheidies has competed in nearly 200 triathlons around the globe. These three-part races involve swimming, biking, and running. He has even taken part in long-distance Ironman triathlons. During the swim and the run, he races while another person helps guide him through the course. And during the bike portion of the race, he rides a tandem (two-seated) bicycle with his guide. Doing this, he has become a seven-time world paratriathlon champion. What's his philosophy? "Until you step outside your comfort box and attempt the uncomfortable, you will never discover your full potential."

and placed eighth overall. In 2004, she made the team again, this time as a 5,000-meter runner.

In addition to her other achievements, Runyan earned two college degrees in educating deaf and blind children. She has long served as an ambassador for the Perkins School for the Blind. (Helen Keller was the school's most famous student.) She tells people that success is a product of effort, not eyesight. "It's a matter of commitment," she said. "Some people have a bad attitude, and that's their disability."

C IS FOR COMEBACK

FEBRUARY 11, 2012 • GETTYSBURG, PENNSYLVANIA, UNITED STATES

It was Senior Day at Gettysburg College. Basketball guard Cory Weissman stepped to the free throw line in the final game of his college career. His team led their rival, Washington College, by 14 points. There were only 16 seconds left in the contest. Weissman's shot wouldn't affect the game's outcome. But even so, everybody in the home crowd desperately hoped that Weissman would make it.

He bounced the ball three times. He flipped it in his hands, and then released it . . .

Three years earlier, as a freshman, Weissman was lifting weights one day. Suddenly his left arm went numb. Soon, his whole left side was paralyzed. Weissman had been born with a problem in his brain. A tangle of arteries and veins burst that day in 2009. He was having a stroke.

46

The condition is fatal about half of the time. Weissman survived. But it was a scary time. He needed a seven-hour surgery. He also spent 11 days at a medical center and then five weeks in a rehabilitation center. On his third day in the rehab center, his mother, Tina, rolled him to an outdoor patio. There was an eight-foot-high basket set up there. With help, Weissman rose from his wheelchair and tossed a few weak right-handed shots toward the hoop. "That's what he needed to do to see himself as himself," said his mom. It became a daily ritual.

Weissman worked hard to heal his body. He also had to overcome frightening seizures. But gradually, he regained his ability to walk and talk. By the time he was a senior, he felt like he was about 90 percent of the way back to full strength. The

most obvious signs of his stroke were a change in his walk and a C-shaped scar on his scalp. With his usual humor, Weissman said it was a C for "Cory." But it also could have stood for "captain." Weissman's teammates were inspired by his hard work and good attitude. They elected him to the captain position before his final year.

In his senior year, Weissman's doctors cleared him for a small amount of sports activity. His dream was to play in just one game. In the year's final contest, Gettysburg coach George Petrie and Washington coach Rob Nugent made it possible. With students chanting his name, Weissman was put into the game for the opening tip-off. He soon headed back to the sidelines. But he felt great. "I finally achieved my goal," he said. "My day was perfect."

And the day wasn't over. With less than a minute to play, Petrie sent him in one more time. Then Nugent signaled his opposing coach. He had an idea. He instructed his players to foul Weissman—very gently. That sent him to the line for two free throws. Here, at last, was his chance to score his first and only points in a college game.

Weismann's first shot missed. It barely even grazed the rim. "I never heard a place get so quiet so quickly," said Petrie. But Weissman was absolutely certain about the next shot. "I saw three years of hard work flash before my eyes," he explained, "and said there's no way this ball's not going in."

Swish.

The shot was chosen as one of ESPN *SportsCenter*'s "Top 10 Plays" of the day.

The win gave Petrie the record for most coaching victories at Gettysburg. He got the game ball as a symbol of his achievement. But Petrie turned to Weissman right away. "Hey," he said, "this is yours."

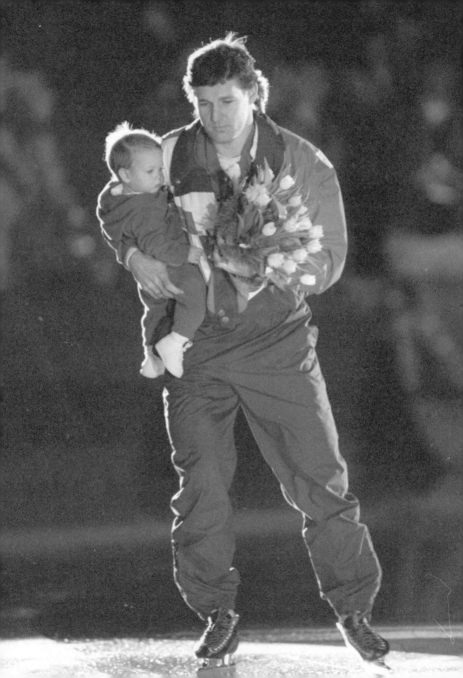

"JUST SKATE"

FEBRUARY 18, 1994 • LILLEHAMMER, NORWAY

For years, speed skater Dan Jansen was known best for heartbreak. The whole world seemed to be pulling for him. Yet he seemed destined to come up just short of his goals. Some people are fated for glory. But others stumble. And some people fall.

Jansen was the youngest of nine children. Their mom was a nurse, and their dad was a police officer. The Jansen family lived in Wisconsin. That's where Jansen's older sister, Jane, first introduced him to speed skating. By the time he was 16, he was a junior world record holder in the sport. Two years later, he made the U.S. Olympic team. At the 1984 Winter Games in what was then Yugoslavia, Jansen finished 16th in the 1,000 meters. In the 500-meter distance, he took fourth place.

Within three years, Jansen was the world's best skater in both events. But as he got ready for the 1988

A NEW GOAL

Cammi Granato scored more goals than any other player in U.S. women's hockey. She won a gold medal at the 1998 Winter Olympics. She even appeared on the cover of a Wheaties box. But off the ice, her life was a bit of a mess. She didn't return emails, pay bills, or clean her house. In 2003, she heard a sports psychologist talking about the symptoms of attention deficit hyperactivity disorder (ADHD). Granato realized she had probably had ADHD all her life. "I'd just assumed I wouldn't finish projects or return calls because I was lazy," she says. "Now I knew the cause and could focus on solutions."

Granato doesn't play competitive hockey anymore, but she did get her life on track. She arranged for automatic online payment of her bills. She made a to-do list and followed it carefully. She got rid of boxes of old papers. Bit by bit, Granato removed most of the clutter from her life. And she learned to appreciate her differences. "ADHD comes with certain strengths and weaknesses that have made me who I am," she says. "I wouldn't trade that for anything."

Winter Olympics in Calgary, Canada, his thoughts were with his sister. At age 27, Jane was battling cancer. Early on the morning of his race, he got a phone call. Jane was dying. He told her that he loved her. He promised her he'd win a gold medal. A few hours later, she passed away.

Jansen's mother urged him to continue in the competition. Jansen agreed. Millions of viewers awaited the dramatic events. But Jansen didn't feel confident. "The day before, there was nothing that was going to make me lose," he said. "On that day, there was nothing that was going to make me win." On the very first turn of the 500-meter race, Jansen fell. Four days later, he was on a world-record pace about halfway through the 1,000 meters. Then he fell again. His Calgary Olympics ended in heartbreak.

In 1992, Jansen tried again. The Winter Olympics in Albertville, France, were coming up. In the months before the Games, Jansen had been setting world records. When he got to France, he was once again favored to win. He felt like it might be his moment. "I was having fun out there," he said. "I wasn't nervous." But he wasn't perfect, either. He came in fourth in the 500 meters, less than one-third of a second behind the winner. A few days later, he faded badly during the final lap of the 1,000 meters. He finished 26th.

Jansen had become a symbol of disappointment.

His next Olympic test came just two years later. The 1994 Winter Olympics were in Lillehammer, Norway. They were Jansen's last chance to prove himself and win gold. But 300 meters into the 500-meter competition, trouble struck again. In speed skating, one little stumble can make all the difference. Jansen briefly lost his balance coming around a turn and dragged his hand on the ice. He wound up in eighth place.

The 1,000-meter race was all that was left. Behind him lay countless hours of practice, four Olympic Games, personal tragedy, and a series of failures witnessed by millions. "Just skate," he told himself. "It'll be over soon." Jansen sped around the ice faster than ever. He nearly slipped at one point—but this time, he regained his balance. When he glided across the finish line, he looked up at the clock. He had beaten the world record by .11 seconds.

Moments later, in front of 10,000 screaming fans, the gold-medal winner skated a victory lap. He carried his eight-month-old daughter in his arms. Her name? Jane.

ON TARGET

SEPTEMBER 2005 • MASSA-CARRERA, ITALY

Bull's-eye! Melanie Clarke's aim was perfect. The 21-year-old British archer had just shot an arrow into the center of the target. Not only that, but she had also achieved what she called "a dream come true." She was in New York City competing in the World Archery Championships against able-bodied opponents.

Clarke (who goes by Mel) competed while sitting in a wheelchair. A decade earlier, she had what seemed like an average knee injury. But it led to a serious infection. Clarke was in and out of the hospital for months. Doctors finally figured out that she had a painful kind of arthritis. They told her she would probably always have to walk with crutches. And for long distances, she would need a wheelchair. "It was a blow," she recalled. "But I was determined not to waste my life."

A few years later, when Clarke was 16, she took up the sport of archery. At first, she couldn't even hit the target. But she practiced often. And she improved remarkably. Eventually, Clarke earned a spot on England's disabled archery team. At the 2002 European Championships, she won a gold medal. Next she was picked to represent her country at the able-bodied championships in New York.

But just after she recorded that bull's-eye, she felt a sharp pain in her chest. She began to feel dizzy in the hot sun and decided to rest in the shade. Suddenly, everything went dark.

Clarke woke up in a hospital three weeks later. She was using a ventilator to breathe and was being fed through a tube. She was permanently blind in her right eye. And she was paralyzed from the waist down.

Clarke had Lyme disease. It was probably caused by a tick bite. The tick carried a certain bacteria that poisoned Clarke's nervous system. Once again, she got discouraging news from her doctors. They told her

ARMLESS ARCHER

In archery, athletes have to use their arms and hands very precisely. Matt Stutzman was born without any arms. Yet at the 2012 London Paralympic Games, he won a silver medal in archery. How does he do it? The 29-year-old American places the arrow with his left foot. He aims the bow with his right foot. Then he pulls back the cord with his teeth and releases it. After he learned how to do that, it's hardly surprising that he also cooks, hunts, fishes, drives a car, and changes the diapers of his three children. Stutzman calls himself "the Armless Archer." He says, "My goal was to inspire somebody, even if it was just one person, with my positive attitude. Never say never."

she'd probably never be able to shoot another arrow. "I shed plenty of tears of frustration," she recalled. "But I loved archery, and I wasn't about to let an insect bite take away my passion."

So about five months later, she picked up her bow again. Clarke's blind eye had been her aiming eye. So she learned how to change her shooting style. Sitting in her wheelchair, she tilted her head back to make best use of her working eye. And she picked a new target to aim for—the 2005 World Disabled Archery Games in Massa-Carrera, Italy.

Just two years earlier, Clarke's doctors had feared she only had 24 hours to live. Could she really return to the top of her sport?

Bull's-eye. At the 2005 games, Clarke took gold in her category.

Three years later, Clarke won a bronze medal at the 2008 Summer Paralympics in Beijing, China. In 2012, she competed in the Paralympics again—this time, in her home country. The championship came down to the final arrow, and Clarke wound up with a silver medal. But she knew how far she had come, and she was thrilled. "It's been a rocky road," she said, "but every single minute has been worth it now."

CONQUERING A CONTINENT

JANUARY 22, 2012 • ANTARCTICA

Felicity Aston knew exactly what she wanted after her record-setting journey. "A very long, very hot shower," she said. "It's something I haven't had in quite a long time."

Fifty-nine days, to be exact. That's how long it took Aston to become the first human to ski solo across

Antarctica without help from kites or machines. At 34 years old, the British adventurer used only her own muscles and mental resolve. For nearly two months, Aston dragged 187 pounds of supplies behind her on two sleds. She crossed 1,084 miles of ice and snow. Her diet was mostly freeze-dried food, and she battled through temperatures well below freezing. Sometimes it was as cold as 22 degrees below zero. And she was all alone.

Aston started at a location called the Ross Ice Shelf. From there, she traveled up Leverett Glacier. As she headed across the glacier, the wind blew so hard that she thought her tent was going to rip apart. Then, as she crossed the Transantarctic Mountains, her two lighters suddenly stopped working. Aston was in trouble. The lighters were how she lit her stove. She also used them to melt snow for drinking water. Aston needed fire to survive. She did have a box of safety matches—exactly 46 of them. She used them very carefully, hoping they would last. Finally, as she came down out of the mountains, her lighters began to work again.

WISE WORDS

"Sweat plus sacrifice equals success."
—Charlie Finley, former Oakland A's owner

Aston next crossed the vast central plain, fighting against constant headwinds. At last, on December 20, 2011, Aston arrived at the South Pole. The stop was one of only two points in her journey where she got fresh supplies.

Aston got to the pole six days after a big anniversary. One hundred years earlier, Norwegian explorer Roald Amundsen was the first person ever to reach the globe's southernmost point. He did it on December 14, 1911. But Amundsen had traveled with four teammates and more than 50 dogs. Aston was by herself. And she went far past the pole. In fact, she went all the way to the other side of the continent. After all, she had a deadline to meet. She had to catch the last flight out of Antarctica before the harsh winter set in.

Aston had faced tough challenges before. She had raced in the Canadian Arctic, trekked across the

Sahara Desert, and skied along a frozen Siberian river. But in Antarctica, she learned that her biggest hardship wasn't physical. It was mental. Loneliness was the enemy. "Being alone sounds like such a simple thing," says Aston. "But when was the last time you went a whole day without seeing any person?" During her trek, Aston was alone for weeks.

Her happiest moment came near the end of the trip. The weather was stormy as she arrived at a place called Hercules Inlet. She knew she was close to her destination, but she didn't know exactly *how* close. Then the clouds parted. In the distance, Aston saw what she described as "fat, little triangles on the horizon." Those triangles were the coastal mountains. "I just stopped in my tracks, and burst into tears," she recalled. It took another four days for her to reach the coast—where she arrived three days ahead of schedule.

Along the way, Aston had learned a lot about pushing her limits. She explains that whatever challenge you're facing, "if you can just find a way to keep going, then you will discover that you have potential within yourself that you never realized. At some point in the future you'll look back and just be amazed at how far you've come."

THE MATCH THAT WOULDN'T END

JUNE 24, 2010 • WIMBLEDON, ENGLAND

When American John Isner and Frenchman Nicolas Mahut played each other at the 2010 Wimbledon Championships, no one expected a historic match. But they got one. The worst thing about it? Somebody had to lose.

63

It was only a first-round meeting on Court 18 at the All England Lawn Tennis Club. And the players weren't especially well known. But in the face of total exhaustion, both men refused to back down. That determination made their battle one of the most celebrated tennis matches in history.

It started normally enough. The match began on a Tuesday evening at Wimbledon. Isner won the first set 6–4. Mahut took the second one 6–3. They split sets

EXTRA EXTRA INNINGS

The longest professional baseball game ever played began on April 18, 1981. The minor league Rochester (New York) Red Wings were facing the Pawtucket (Rhode Island) Red Sox. After nine innings, the game was tied 1–1. After 10 more innings, it was still 1–1. Each team scored a run in the 21st inning—and then they played another 11 scoreless innings. Finally, at 4:07 AM on April 19, the game was put on hold after 32 innings. Just 19 fans were still watching. The game started up again 55 days later. In the very first inning, after 882 pitches had been thrown to 246 batters, Pawtucket won 3–2.

three and four, each man winning once in a tiebreaker.
A fifth and final set was about to begin. At that point,
officials paused play because of darkness. Amazingly,
the match wasn't even close to over.

The next day, the two men were tied 6–6 in the
final set. That's when things got really interesting.
Wimbledon rules state that there is no tiebreaker
in the fifth set. The victor must win by at least two
games. At that point, neither Isner nor Mahut had bro-
ken the other's serve since the second set. (Breaking
the serve means winning a game in which the opponent is serving the ball.) One of them would have to
do it for the match to end. But it didn't happen.

Soon, Isner and Mahut were tied 8–8. Then 12–12.
Then 15–15. Surely, one of them would break eventually! But neither did. It was 20–20, 25–25, 30–30. Each
player somehow found energy to match the other's.
Hours and hours into the second day of play, the score-
board read 36–36 . . . then 42–42 . . . then 48–48. After
seven hours and six minutes of play on Wednesday
alone, the match was put on hold overnight once
again. The score was tied at 59–59 in that fifth set.
By then, said Isner, "I was completely delirious."

The two tired men returned on Thursday afternoon to finish the epic match. Three-time Wimbledon champion John McEnroe grabbed a seat, hoping to see history unfold. "I had to come pay my respects," he said. Isner and Mahut played another 20 games that day. That's like playing two more full sets! But they just kept tying. Finally, a winner emerged. It had taken 11 hours and five minutes of play. And it happened nearly 48 hours after the match began. This made their match the longest in pro tennis history.

Up to then, the players had played a mind-boggling 711 points in the last set. Mahut had racked up 365, while Isner had 345. But Isner won the most important point of all—the last one. He hit a winning backhand down the line and the match came to an end. The final tally: 6–4, 3–6, 6–7, 7–6 . . . 70–68. The fifth set alone was longer than any five-set *match* ever played in pro tennis.

As the crowd cheered, the 6-foot-9 Isner fell to his back on the court. Then he stood right up and rushed to the net. Usually, the opponents shake hands after a match. This time, the two competitors shared a heartfelt hug. "We played the greatest match ever, in

the greatest place to play tennis," said
Mahut. "I thought he would make a
mistake. I waited for that moment, and
it never came."

FINISHING TOUCH

AUGUST 3, 1992 • BARCELONA, SPAIN

It was the slowest 400-meter run in Olympic history. It was also one of the most memorable.

Derek Redmond settled into the starting blocks for the 400-meter semifinals at the 1992 Summer Olympics in Barcelona. The 26-year-old British sprinter felt fit and ready. Sure, an Achilles tendon injury had forced him to drop out of a race at the Olympics four years earlier. And yes, since then he'd had eight operations on that injury and others. But in Barcelona, he had the fastest time in the first round of competition. He felt like it was his moment.

Redmond got off to a fast start in the semifinal heat. But about halfway through the race he heard a loud pop. Then he felt terrible pain in his right leg. "I thought I'd been shot," he said later. Actually, he had torn his right hamstring. His leg was barely working. As he grimaced in pain and hobbled to a halt, the thousands of spectators groaned. For several moments, Redmond kneeled down in pain, his head in his hands. A disappointed British television announcer declared, "The jinx has struck again."

As the other seven runners raced into the distance, Redmond fell to his back on the track. He was completely disheartened. But then he sat up and watched his competitors finish the race. Redmond straightened with determination. He decided that he was going to finish, too—no matter what. Race officials tried to help him off the track, but he ignored them. He rose and began to hobble forward. With his right leg so badly hurt, he basically hopped on his one good leg. As spectators realized what he was doing, they began to applaud. Still, Redmond felt devastated. "Everything I had worked for was finished. I hated everybody. I hated the world. I hated hamstrings. I hated it all," he said. But he kept moving. "Then," he said, "with 100 meters to go, I felt a hand on my shoulder."

It was his dad.

Jim Redmond later said that as he saw his son struggling, he just knew "it was my duty to help." He rushed down from the stands, charged past security guards, and ran to his son's side. He grabbed Derek's hand and threw a supportive arm around him. He told him he didn't have to keep going. But Derek refused to quit. So, slowing to a walk, father and son finished a full lap around the track together. As they reached the home stretch, the crowd stood and clapped. Derek Redmond leaned his head on his father's shoulder and began to cry.

WISE WORDS

"It does not matter how many times you get knocked down, but how many times you get up."
—Vince Lombardi, Hall of Fame Green Bay Packers coach

Runners aren't allowed to have help during a race. So in the official records, Redmond was disqualified. He was listed as "DID NOT FINISH." But he certainly did finish. "I intended to go over the line with him," said his father afterward. "We started his career together. I think we should finish it together."

Indeed, Redmond would never sprint at the world-class level again. Instead, he moved on to other sports. He played rugby and raced motorcycles. He even earned a spot on England's national basketball team. Later, he became a motivational speaker. And his dad? He was one of the runners who carried the Olympic flame during the torch relay for the 2012 Summer Olympics in London. He carried the Olympic torch just as his love and support had carried his son to the finish line two decades earlier.

HARD TO TAKE DOWN

MARCH 19, 2011 • PHILADELPHIA, PENNSYLVANIA, UNITED STATES

It isn't often that a college wrestler gets a standing ovation from an audience of sports superstars. But there they were, on their feet—Dirk Nowitzki and Danica Patrick, Serena Williams and Aaron Rodgers, and many others. They were cheering for the winner of the Jimmy V Award for Perseverance at the 2011 ESPY Awards in Los Angeles. Talk show host Jay Leno had presented the award. It was named for former college basketball coach Jim Valvano. Valvano lost his life to cancer in 1993, but he won the hearts of millions with his never-give-up attitude. "Some people spend their entire lives wishing for amazing things they'll never get," Leno told the celebrity audience. "Others just focus on doing amazing things with whatever they have."

Then the wrestler, the winner of the award, walked to the center of the stage. He used crutches. He has used them all his life.

Anthony Robles was born July 20, 1988, without a right leg. Doctors weren't sure why. His mother, Judy,

WHAT A KICK

Tom Dempsey was born without toes on his right foot and without fingers on his right hand. He went on to be a football star. He was a placekicker. Dempsey wore a special shoe with a flattened toe surface. Over 11 seasons, he played for five NFL teams. But it was in his second season that he made history. On November 8, 1970, he kicked a 63-yard field goal. The play lifted Dempsey's New Orleans Saints to a last-second 19–17 victory over the Detroit Lions. "The Saints have won! The crowd is wild! Dempsey is being mobbed!" shouted the TV announcer, as Dempsey's teammates celebrated at midfield.

And Dempsey did more than win the game. He made a record-setting kick. Dempsey's field goal was a full seven yards longer than the previous record. And Dempsey's record stood for 43 years. No one would break it until 2013.

decided it didn't really matter to her. "She raised me to believe I could do anything I wanted," Robles says. "Really, I thought I was Superman." Robles also thinks highly of his mom. He tells anyone and everyone he was honored to be her son.

As a child, doctors gave Robles an artificial leg. But he felt like it was clunky and awkward. Whenever his mother wasn't looking, he would try to take it off and hide it. In the end, she left it up to him. He preferred crutches. When he tried to play football in seventh and eighth grade, he dropped the crutches and hopped around the field. Pretty soon he realized football wasn't his game. An older cousin suggested he try wrestling. "I jumped into it," said Robles, "and just fell in love with it."

Wrestling is a sport where leg strength is often crucial. So it didn't start very well for Robles. As a high school freshman in Mesa, Arizona, he won only 5 of 13 matches. He also finished last in a city wrestling tournament. But he kept working. He strengthened his upper body and improved his wrestling technique. And by his junior and senior years, he seemed to be unbeatable. Robles went 96–0, winning two state championships and a national championship. Yet even with this success, many colleges didn't try to recruit him. Most college scouts thought a one-legged wrestler wouldn't do well against top college athletes.

Arizona State University saw the potential in Robles. He earned a spot on their team, and he just got better and better. As a freshman, he went 25–11. As a sophomore and junior, Robles won 61 of 73 matches. Twice he earned All-America honors in the 125-pound weight class. And as a senior, he didn't lose at all. The final competition of his career was at the 2011 NCAA Wrestling Championships in Philadelphia. In that match, Robles defeated the defending national champion and earned an NCAA title of his own. He was also voted the Most Outstanding Wrestler of the tournament.

Of course, his mother was there the whole time. She cheered wildly from the stands. "The pride I feel for him is indescribable," she said. "It's an honor to be Anthony's mom."

FACE TIME

MAY 17, 2010 • NEW BRIGHTON, MINNESOTA, UNITED STATES

Growing up in Minnesota, Robbie Wilhelm was a die-hard sports fan. He read *Sports Illustrated* every week. He had visions of one day seeing his own name in the pages of the magazine, and maybe even his picture. "I always dreamed," he said, "of being in 'Faces in the Crowd.'"

"Faces in the Crowd" is a long-running segment in the magazine. It highlights the accomplishments of

77

six athletes, alongside their smiling faces. More than 17,000 "Faces" have appeared on the page since 1956. Usually, they are little known outside their local area. But many of them eventually emerge as all-stars and

Hall of Famers. In fact, dozens have gone on to grace the cover of the magazine! Quarterback Tim Tebow was mentioned three years before he won college football's Heisman Trophy. Minnesota Twins catcher Joe Mauer was touted for his high school football talent. Figure skater Michelle Kwan appeared when she was just 12 years old. The feature gave readers their first glimpses of golfer Tiger Woods, running back Emmitt Smith, tennis champion John McEnroe, and Olympic track star Jackie Joyner-Kersee.

But what about Robbie Wilhelm? Being a star didn't seem likely for him. His legs had been weakened by polio as a child. As he got older, they only grew weaker. A family friend suggested he try wheelchair basketball. When Wilhelm first took up the game in 2007, he didn't expect much. "I thought it was nothing really that exciting or aggressive," he said. "But you have to witness it to see how intense it is."

The game's rules are similar to standard basketball. And as in standard basketball, the baskets are 10 feet high. But players don't commit traveling violations by walking with the ball. Instead, if they move by touching their wheels twice, they have to dribble, pass, or shoot the ball before they touch the wheels again.

Wilhelm joined a team called the Courage Center Junior Rolling Timberwolves. The team practiced three hours a day, five days a week. Wilhelm worked to perfect his wheelchair moves, strengthen his arms, and improve his shooting from a sitting position. "You need to believe in yourself and have confidence in yourself. It all starts there," he said.

The Junior Rolling Timberwolves won a National Wheelchair Basketball Association varsity title in 2008. They repeated their victory the next year. In 2010, they breezed past the competition to reach the championship again. They would play against a team from California. Because Wilhelm was a senior at Irondale High School, it was his last game with the squad. Soon he would be playing college ball at Southwest Minnesota State University. Hoping to go out on top, he gave it his all—and played one of the best games of his life. Wilhelm and his teammates won by 38 points. Wilhelm's own 32-point performance matched the total of the entire opposing team!

Wilhelm was named tournament MVP (most valuable player). After the game, his coach, Mike Bauler, sent an email to *Sports Illustrated*. Bauler nominated Wilhelm for a spot in "Faces in the Crowd." And when the May 17, 2010, issue of the magazine hit the newsstands, there was Wilhelm. If he stood out a little from the "Crowd," it was only because his smile was just a bit wider than anyone else's.

ATHLETE OF THE YEAR

One of Robbie Wilhelm's champion wheelchair basketball teammates was Thomas Bowlin from St. Paul, Minnesota. Thomas was born with spina bifada. This often-painful disorder affects the spinal cord. Over the years, Thomas faced more than 70 surgeries. By the time he was 13, he needed a wheelchair full time. But he didn't let that stop him from being an athlete. He joined adaptive teams for students with physical disabilities. With these teams, he earned 14 letters in varsity sports. He also won eight all-conference awards. In 2011, he joined a list that includes Hall of Fame baseball players Dave Winfield and Paul Molitor when he was named St. Paul Athlete of the Year. Bowlin was the first adaptive athlete to win this honor.

LITTLE GIANT

FEBRUARY 16, 1984 • SARAJEVO, YUGOSLAVIA

Four-time world champion figure skater Scott Hamilton believes that the hardest jump in his sport is one that follows a fall. "Your confidence is shaken, your timing is obviously off, and that's where you really prove yourself," he said. But he also insists that falling down is good for you. Mistakes will happen. Obstacles will arise. They test your strength. "The longer you lie there, the colder you get," Hamilton says. "So the first thing, and the obvious thing, is to get up."

Hamilton may know this better than anyone. When he was only two years old, he stopped growing. His body wasn't taking nutrition from his food. Doctors couldn't figure out why. Eventually, Hamilton got better. But even as an adult, he only reached a height of 5-foot-2½. At the age of nine, he took up figuring skating. It was a sport where size wasn't an issue. Skating boosted his confidence—in part because he had natural talent. However, training was expensive. To afford it, his mother worked full time. Hamilton's mother had adopted him when he was six weeks old. She continued to work and support her son even while she went through surgery and chemotherapy for cancer. "I thought about all she had gone through to make sure I was given the opportunities," Hamilton said. "I made a vow to myself never to be less than she knew I could be."

BOSTON STRONG

In 2007, Jon Lester pitched nearly six shutout innings in Game 4 of the World Series. That happened just 10 months after Lester finished cancer treatments. So everyone figured he wouldn't be able to top that moment. He earned the victory, and the Boston Red Sox earned the world championship. His teammate Jonathan Papelbon said, "He's definitely an inspiration to all of us. We all go through ups and downs in life, and he went through a really big down in life and was able to fight through it and come back." The very next season, Lester pitched a no-hitter—the first by a Boston left-hander in 52 years.

Hamilton worked hard to keep that promise. He dedicated himself to training. In 1980, he earned a spot on the U.S. Olympic figure skating team. He wasn't in the running for a medal. But his grit impressed his teammates. They chose him to carry the U.S. flag during the opening ceremony of the Olympic Games. He finished fifth that winter, but the next year he won the U.S. Championships. He never lost another major amateur competition. From 1982 to 1984, he earned U.S. and world titles. Hamilton capped off his amateur career with a gold medal at the 1984 Winter Games in Yugoslavia. (Since then Yugoslavia has been divided into the nations of Bosnia and Herzegovina, Croatia, Kosovo, Macedonia, Montenegro, Serbia, and Slovenia.)

Afterward, Hamilton turned professional. As a pro, he won several more championships. He also changed the sport by creating a traveling tour. The tour came to be called Stars on Ice. But in 1997, he faced a big fall. He was shocked to find out that he had cancer. Hamilton stayed determined. He pledged to get back up. "I can overcome this disease and be back on the ice," he said at the time. Within a year, he did just that. He weathered the difficult treatment, trained hard, and got back to skating.

He got up after another fall seven years later, when doctors found and removed a brain tumor. He rose up once more in 2010, when doctors took out another tumor, along with a weak, enlarged blood vessel. That surgery took away most of the vision in his right eye. Still, Hamilton inspired friends and strangers. He stayed optimistic and full of good humor. He even joked that he had found a new hobby—"collecting life-threatening illnesses." He devoted himself to raising funds for cancer research through the Scott Hamilton CARES Initiative.

"Everything that I've ever been able to accomplish in skating and in life has come out of adversity and perseverance," he said. "All the things that were meant to kind of pull me down made me better."

TECH TRIUMPH

DECEMBER 18, 2008 • WINSTED, CONNECTICUT, UNITED STATES

In the late 2000s, one basketball team in Connecticut was riding high. The University of Connecticut women's basketball team won a record 90 games in a row from 2008 to 2010. Those wins included two back-to-back undefeated championship seasons. But for nearly 19 years, a high school girls' team in the same state was at the other end of the spectrum. The basketball squad from Oliver T. Wolcott Technical High School played 265 games between February 1990 and December 2008. They didn't win a single one.

Technical schools draw students who want to learn a trade. For much of the year, Wolcott students spend only a few hours a day at school. The rest of the day, they go to paid jobs, working at everything from auto repair to medical technology. Many students choose this chance to earn money instead of playing their favorite sport. This always made it difficult to

"Obstacles don't have to stop you. If you run into a wall, don't turn around and give up. Figure out how to climb it, go through it, or work around it."

—Michael Jordan, NBA Hall of Famer

put together a strong team. Plus, Wolcott decided not to play in a division specifically for tech schools. Instead, they played in the close-to-home Berkshire Division, and faced tougher teams from area high schools.

In 2007, Mark Eucalitto took over as coach of the Wolcott team. As usual, his first group of girls went 0–20. But the next year, he sensed that maybe—just maybe—his team might be able to end its losing streak. On December 18, 2009, the Wildcats traveled to the town of Winsted to take on Gilbert High School. It was their third game of the season. "Losing is not an option," Eucalitto told his players. "We are not coming home without a victory."

Of course, losing had been just about the *only* option for Wolcott for almost two decades. Would this be any different?

Things started well for the Wildcats. After one quarter against Gilbert, Wolcott led 11–4. After two quarters, the Wildcats led 28–20. Could this be the night the streak ended?

The third quarter seemed to suggest otherwise. Wolcott scored only five points. Gilbert tied the game. It was 33–33 with just eight minutes to play. You might think years of losing could turn into a habit. But hope leads to perseverance. And the Wolcott players never lost hope. "We had so much adrenaline pumping from pep talks from coaches and teachers and everybody," said senior Alyssa Paniati, who scored 18 points against Gilbert. "It definitely felt like an opportunity."

The Wildcats grabbed that opportunity. They outscored Gilbert 21–10 in the fourth quarter. Final score: Wolcott 54, Gilbert 43. "Tech! Tech! Tech!" the girls shouted, joining for a group hug. "We have been working really hard," said Wolcott senior Sarah Zbell afterward. "We knew it was going to pay off."

Wolcott went home with a victory. And they didn't stop there. They also won at home the very next night. Three years later, for the 2011–2012 season, the Wildcats moved into the Constitution State Conference. In that division, they competed mostly against other tech teams. They played well enough to qualify for the state tournament. It was a far cry from the winless Wildcats of old. The big reason? Simple, according to new coach Brian Hurlock: "They started to believe."

HIS NAME IS PRIDE

SEPTEMBER 17, 1993 • MONTREAL, CANADA

It was a key mid-September baseball series. The
Montreal Expos (now the Washington Nationals)
were battling the Philadelphia Phillies for first place.
Late in the game, Montreal was losing 7–4. With two
men on base, pinch-hitter Curtis Pride walked to the
plate. It would be only the second at-bat of his major
league career.

Pride's journey to the Big Show had been a big deal. From the beginning, his talent rang out loud and clear—even if he couldn't hear it. Before Pride had reached his first birthday, doctors had confirmed his parents' fears. Their son was deaf. But for John and Sallie Pride, he was their pride and joy. And they taught him that hearing loss didn't have to mean a loss of self-esteem. "I never had a hearing impaired role model when I was younger," Pride explained. "My parents were my role models because they taught me to believe in myself."

Pride had 95 percent hearing loss. He used the five percent he had left to help him speak. He also learned to read lips. And he thrived as an athlete. Sports came naturally to Pride. During his four years at College of William & Mary, he was an All-American soccer player. He was also a point guard on the basketball team. He spent his summers playing minor league baseball as an outfielder. But Pride was proudest of the fact that he graduated.

On the diamond, Pride compensated for his hearing loss with his sharp eyesight and his speed. Outfielders often listen to the crack of the bat to judge how hard a ball is hit. Pride paid attention to the angle at which it left the bat. After a total of eight minor league seasons during and after college, he earned a call-up to the Expos. On September 14, 1993, Pride became the first hearing impaired major leaguer in nearly 50 years. He was 24 years old.

Just three days later, he made that pinch-hit appearance against the Phillies. Expos manager Felipe Alou had been getting letters and phone calls from people who were hearing impaired. They were asking him to give Pride a chance. But Alou's decision to put Pride in the game didn't have anything to do with his hearing.

It was all about baseball. "There was something in the delivery of the pitcher," he said, "that made me think Curtis could hit him." Pride slapped the very first pitch to the wall for a two-run double.

It was the beginning of another journey. Pride went on to play for 6 different teams over 11 major league seasons. He also did much more. He later became head baseball coach at Gallaudet University. The school is for students who are deaf or hard of hearing. Pride also started the Together with Pride Foundation to support programs for hearing impaired children. And he was selected to the President's Council on Fitness, Sports, and Nutrition.

SENDING SIGNALS

Like Curtis Pride, William Hoy was hearing impaired. As a kid, some classmates cruelly nicknamed him "Dummy" because of his hearing loss. But he turned out to be one of the best center fielders of his time. Hoy played in the major leagues from 1888 to 1902. He recorded a .288 career batting average and 597 stolen bases. As a rookie, Hoy led the league with 82 stolen bases. The next year, he set a major league record by throwing out three runners at home plate in a single game. But Hoy's most lasting mark on the game may be the hand signals he developed. Hoy communicated with his teammates and coaches using these signals. Many people believe that they developed into the hand signals still used in baseball games today.

But if any moment represented the obstacles Pride had overcome, it was that moment when he stood on second base after knocking in two runs. Montreal fans rose to their feet to honor Pride's achievement. They realized that this was more than just a clutch swing or a rookie's first hit. It was perseverance on display. The third-base coach called timeout and walked across the diamond. He pointed out what Pride hadn't noticed: The 47,757 fans were cheering like crazy. It was time for him to tip his cap.

SELECTED BIBLIOGRAPHY

Anderson, Kelli. "Putting Mettle to the Pedal." *Sports Illustrated*. September 17, 2012.

Associated Press. "Breland Ready to Focus on Future." ESPN *sports.espn.go.com/ncw/news/story?id=4708733*. December 3, 2009 (accessed April 24, 2012).

Associated Press. "Felicity Aston Skis Across Antarctica." *USA Today. usatoday30.usatoday.com/news/world/story/2012-01-23/woman-skis-antarctica/52757144/1*. January 24, 2012 (accessed April 21, 2012).

Associated Press. "Isner Beats Mahut in Epic 11-Hour Match." ESPN. *sports.espn.go.com/sports/tennis/wimbledon10/news/story?id=5322284*. June 24, 2010 (accessed April 21, 2012).

"Dewey Bozella Wins Pro Boxing Debut." ESPN. *espn.go.com/los-angeles/story/_/id/7108340/exonerated-ex-con-dewey-bozella-wins-pro boxing-debut-52*. October 16, 2011 (accessed April 21, 2012).

Drohan, Kerry. "A Champion Passes the Torch." *The Boston Globe*. October 3, 1999.

Garber, Greg. "A Story of Triumph, Sportsmanship." ESPN. *espn.go.com/mens-college-basketball/story/_/id/7607463*. February 24, 2012 (accessed March 25, 2012).

Herzog, Brad. *The Sports 100: The One Hundred Most Important People in American Sports History*. New York: Macmillan, 1995.

Honeyball, Lee. "I Hated the World. Then I Felt a Hand on My Shoulder." *The Guardian.* January 7, 2007.

Longman, Jere. "Runner with Impaired Sight Sets Olympic Berth as a Goal." *The New York Times.* April 19, 2000.

Morfit, Cameron. "Erik Compton—on His Third Heart—Has Shown More Mettle than Anyone in the Game." Golf.com. *www.golf.com/tour-and-news/erik-compton-151-his-third-heart-151-has-shown-more-mettle-anyone-game.* September 8, 2011 (accessed April 22, 2012).

Riley, Lori. "Wolcott Tech Girls Basketball Team Leaves Winless Days Behind." *The Hartford Courant.* January 22, 2012.

Wallechinsky, David. *The Complete Book of the Olympics.* New York: Penguin Books, 1988.

Wise, Mike. "Honorable Move Made in a Snap." *The Washington Post.* February 26, 2006.

INDEX

A

Abbott, Jim, 5–8
Adaptive athletes, 81
ADHD, See Attention deficit
    hyperactivity disorder
    (ADHD)
Ali, Muhammad, 24
Alou, Felipe, 92
Amputations, See Limbs, loss of
Amundsen, Roald, 61
Archery, 55–58
Arizona State University, 76
Aston, Felicity, 59–62
Arthritis, 55–58
Attention deficit hyperactivity
    disorder (ADHD), 52
Auto racing, 20, 28

B

Baseball, 5–8, 64, 84, 90–94
Basketball
  men's, 46–49
  wheelchair, 77–81
  women's, 37–39, 87–89
Bauler, Mike, 80
Blindness, See Vision loss

Boston Red Sox, 84
Bowlin, Thomas, 81
Boxing, 23–26
Bozella, Dewey, 23–26
Brain tumors, 86
Brands Hatch road-racing course,
    27, 29
Breland, Jessica, 37–39

C

Cancer, 37–39, 84, 85
Championship Auto Racing
    Teams (CART) series, 28
Children's Miracle Network
    Classic golf tournament, 17
Clarke, Melanie, 55–58
Cleveland Indians, 5
College of William & Mary, 91
Compton, Erik, 15–18
Connecticut Sun, 39
Courage Center Junior Rolling
    Timberwolves (Minnesota),
    79–80
Croizon, Philippe, 33
Cross-country skiing, 59–62

D

Deafness, *See* Hearing loss
Dempsey, Tom, 74
Detroit Lions, 74
Distance running, 10, 40–45
Dyslexia, 19–22

E

Ederle, Gertrude, 31–35
Endurance
  baseball longest game, 64
  cross-country skiing, 59–62
  swimming, 31–35
  tennis, 63–67
English Channel, swimming,
  31–35
ESPY Awards (2011), 73
Eucalitto, Mark, 88
European Archery
  Championships, 56

F

Fencing, 19–22
Figure skating, 83–86
Finley, Charlie, 61
Football, 74

G

Gallaudet University, 92
Gettysburg College, 46, 48–49
Gilbert High School (Connecticut),
  88–89
Golf, 15–18
Granato, Cammi, 52

H

Hamilton, Scott, 83–86
Handcycling, 1–2, 27–30
Hearing loss, 35, 90–94
Heart transplants, 15–18
Heptathlon, 43
Hockey, women's, 52
Hodgkin's lymphoma, 37–39
Honda Classic golf tournament,
  18
Hopkins, Larry, 26
Hoy, William, 93
Hurlock, Brian, 89

I

Ice skating
  figure skating, 83–86
  speed skating, 51–54
Injuries, overcoming
  hamstring tear, 69–71
  loss of legs, 27–30
  paralysis, 1–2
Innocence Project, 25–26
Irondale High School (Minnesota),
  80
Ironman World Championship,
  2, 44
Isner, John, 63–67

J

James, Ricky, 1–2
James E. Sullivan Memorial
  Award, 8
Jansen, Dan, 51–54
Jessica Breland Comeback Kids
  fund, 39

Jimmy V Award for Perseverance, 73

Jordan, Michael, 88

Joyner-Kersee, Jackie, 79

K

Keller, Helen, 45

Kwan, Michelle, 79

L

Lasorda, Tommy, 10

Learning disabilities
    attention deficit hyperactivity disorder, 52
    dyslexia, 19–22

Leno, Jay, 73

Lester, Jon, 84

Limbs, loss of
    archery, 57
    auto racing, 28
    handcycling, 27–30
    pitching, 5–8
    swimming, 33

Lombardi, Vince, 71

Loneliness, overcoming, 59–62

Lyme disease, 57–58

M

Mahut, Nicholas, 63–67

Mauer, Joe, 79

McEnroe, John, 79

Mexico Open golf tournament, 18

Mickelson, Phil, 18

Mills, Billy, 9–13

Minnesota Lynx, 39

Molitor, Paul, 81

Montreal Expos, 90, 92, 94

Motocross, 1

N

National Football League, 74

National Wheelchair Basketball Association tournament, 80

NCAA Wrestling Championship (2011), 76

New Orleans Saints, 74

New York Liberty, 39

New York Yankees, 5, 8

Nugent, Rob, 48–49

O

Obama, Barack, 26

Oberg, Shay, 7

Oliver T. Wolcott Technical School (Connecticut), 87–89

Olsen, Merlin, 29

Olympic Games
    summer 1924, 32
    summer 1960, 12
    summer 1964, 10
    summer 1988, 8, 21
    summer 1992, 21, 69–71
    summer 2000, 41, 44–45
    summer 2004, 45
    summer 2012, 71
    winter 1980, 85
    winter 1984, 85
    winter 1988, 51, 52, 53
    winter 1992, 53
    winter 1994, 54

P

Paige, Satchel, 38
Pan-American Games, 21, 41
Paniati, Alyssa, 89
Papelbon, Jonathan, 84
Paralympics
    summer 1992, 41
    summer 2008, 58
    summer 2012, 29, 30, 57, 58
Paralysis, 1–2
Paratriathlon, 44
Pawtucket (Rhode Island) Red
    Sox, 64
Pechinsky, Joe, 20–21
Perkins School for the Blind, 45
Perseverance, characteristics of,
    2–3
Personal loss, 51–54
Petrie, George, 48–49
Pham, Si, 17
Philadelphia Phillies, 90, 92
Pitchers, 5–8, 84
Placekicking, 74
Polio, 9–13, 77–80
President's Council on Fitness,
    Sports, and Nutrition, 92
Pride, Curtis, 90–92, 94
Pride, John and Sallie, 91
Prison time, 23–26

R

Redmond, Derek, 69–71
Redmond, Jim, 70–71
Robinson, Jackie, 11
Robles, Anthony, 73–76

Robles, Judy, 74–75, 76
Rochester (New York) Red Wings,
    64
Rome Marathon, 29
Rudolph, Wilma, 9–13
Running, See Track and field
Runyan, Marla, 40–45

S

Scheidies, Aaron, 44
Scott Hamilton CARES Initiative,
    86
Self-esteem, 19–22
Skiing, cross-country, 59–62
Sliney, Molly Sullivan, 19–22
Smith, Emmitt, 79
Speed skating, 51–54
Spina bifida, 81
Sports Illustrated, 77–78, 80
Sprinting, 9–13, 69–71
Stargardt disease, 40–45
Stars on Ice, 85
Stewart, Jackie, 20
Stroke, 46–49
Stutzman, Matt, 57
Swimming, 31–35

T

Tebow, Tim, 79
Tennis, 63–67
Together with Pride Foundation,
    92
Track and field
    distance running, 40–45
    heptathlon, 43
    sprinting, 9–13, 69–71

Triathlon, 1–2, 44
Twin Cities Marathon, 41

U

University of Connecticut, 87
University of Michigan, 6
University of Notre Dame, 20
U.S. Open (golf), 18

V

Valvano, Jim, 73
Venice Marathon, 29
Vision loss, 40–45, 86

W

Washington College, 46, 48–49
Weissman, Cory, 46–49
Wheelchair basketball, 77–81
Wilhelm, Robbie, 77–80
Wilma Rudolph Courage Award,
        12–13
Wimbledon Championships,
        2010, 63–67

Winfield, Dave, 81
Wolcott Technical School
        (Connecticut), 87–89
Women's National Basketball
        Association (WNBA), 37–39
Women's Sports Foundation,
        12–13
Wooden, John, 48
Woods, Tiger, 79
World Archery Championships,
        55
World Disabled Archery Games,
        58
World Routing Car
        Championship, 28
Wrestling, 73–76

Z

Zanardi, Alex, 27–30
Zbell, Sarah, 89

ABOUT THE AUTHOR

Brad Herzog is the author of more than 30 books for children, including more than two dozen sports books. He has also published three travel memoirs in addition to a fourth book for adults, *The Sports 100*, which ranks and profiles the 100 most important people in U.S. sports history. For his freelance magazine writing (including *Sports Illustrated* and *Sports Illustrated Kids*), Brad has won three gold medals from the Council for Advancement and Support of Education. Brad travels all over the United States visiting schools as a guest author. His website, **bradherzog.com**, includes information about his other books and about his school visits and presentations. Brad lives on California's Monterey Peninsula with his wife and two sons.

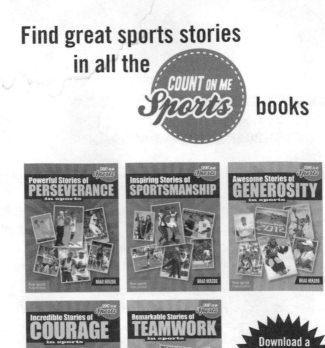